UNPLANNED TRIPS

AF665098

Manash Mahanta

BookLeaf Publishing
India | USA | UK

UNPLANNED TRIPS

© 2024 Manash Mahanta

All rights reserved.

No part of this publication may be reproduced, stored in a retrieval system, or transmitted, in any form or by any means, electronic, mechanical, photocopying, recording or otherwise, without the prior written permission of the presenters and the author.

Manash Mahanta asserts the moral right to be identified as the author of this work.

Presentation by *BookLeaf Publishing*

Web: www.bookleafpub.com

E-mail: info@bookleafpub.com

ISBN: 9789363318021

First edition 2024

"Dedicated to my parents

for always letting me be and make choices,

however tough that may have been to them.

Indebted!"

ACKNOWLEDGEMENT

Gratitude is the only form of acknowledgement that I can humbly offer—not merely for this book but for how I have been all these years. Grateful!

Starts with my unassuming parents, sister, and her lovely family. The arc then meets my better-half, who has natural intent and energy for strong filial bonds and friendly love. My pets that have come, gone, and stayed forever etched.

Cousins, with whom, I have close childhood memories and kindred spirit for life. Girlfriends, who came to my life, played crucial roles in my evolution beyond anything. Places lived and visited: the people, relationships, cultures and aesthetics that I became an instrument to observe and absorb.

Friends met from childhood till today—in our yards, villages, towns, cities, sports, schools, colleges, professions, addas, parties, daily lives, good times and tough times. Being very poor at keeping in touch and mingling with people regularly, some friendships over the years have changed conduct. But at a one on one level, in my mind, there is always an organic connection like we just met yesterday. I have seen close brothers and guiding mentors in a couple of friends. Fortunate!

Lessons that I am trying to learn and unlearn. Talking about lessons and their blessings—teachers and guides—without whose mentoring I would not be the person to be able to be writing this piece of acknowledgement—thank you, sincerely.

Last but definitely not the least—
nature and its wonders,
the unknowns and imagination,
ordinary day-to-day life, God of everything—
three cheers of acknowledgement...

The movies watched, music listened to, books read, paintings not understood, people heard, eyes seen—you are unwittingly my co-creators in this trip that is becoming a book.

My publishers—the design, editing, compliance, helpdesk, and publishing teams for collaborating so iteratively in bringing out my first book—much much thanks.

PREFACE

'Unplanned Trips' have been a major characteristic of our very being. Ranging from road trips per se to inner trips that intrinsically define, defy and inspire to evolve who we are.

Mind over matter—education options, career choices, relationship leaps of faith—I have mostly been a human who did not plan his trips.

The experiences met in this habit—
some physical, sensory;
some mental, cognitive;
some emotional, imaginary;
some virtual, momentary;
some purposeful, soulful;
some aesthetic, magical;
some humble, fulfilling;
some seemingly real,
some utter surreal,
some searching-for-meanings,
some blissfully-oblivious…
—have all contributed in major and minor roles to bringing this book.

Hopefully, 'Unplanned Trips' would be able to find some relevance in your life. Let me know how your trips were.

Bon voyage!

………

………

HOW ARE YOU?

Sultry summer evening—
On a rendezvous with his own tired mind
an old man, obliviously, sat by a river to unwind.

"How are you?"
—a voice that felt he heard.

"How are you?"
—the stranger river there asked.

Silence came there, all images were gone.
The busy port vanished, all people gone.
Just the river flowing and old man alone.

"Daily,
casually,
isn't that what
you keep asking
one another
all the time?"

"Yet,
ironically,
don't you really
crave for it
on times
that nobody asks?"

Silence was broken by the conversing river.
A sharp arrow hit the pain and felt better.
Old man felt his fatigue was his answer.
He felt this was how he was. Fatigued.

He asked the river this time,
"Even you must be craving."
"So, how are you?"

River remained silent.
Time stood bent.
River became curvier.
And curvier. And curvier.
Became a girl,
a woman,
a lady,
an old lady!

Old man became a sea.
Old lady became a beach.
Imageries returned soon.
People, voices, ships, the port…
and the horizon
with sun and moon.

FRACTIONS OF A STORY

Fractions of a story
sometimes fuller than the whole…
Who knows what
could be a jigsaw piece's role…

In the magic of poor light
and low pixels—
which picture
is not a picture?
However silent
noisy, blurry, absent—
a story nevertheless,
a picture nonetheless.

When hearts, in a dark well, shine bright—
curves and shades find their own-grown light.
Fractions of a story
sometimes fuller than the whole…
Who knows what
could be a jigsaw piece's role!

THE FIRSTS

It's a world of wonders,
Change of temperatures,
Unknown shapes and faces,
Little-known sounds and voices…
The day in a new world has dawned,
A newborn just cried and yawned.
From the mother's womb,
To some hospital room;
The first journey—
A happy journey.

The touch of tiny hands,
The first loving embrace.
Sweet comfort of mother's milk,
Tender bonding softer than silk.

Times pass, baby's first steps come;
Rise, fall, rise again, they walk some.
Newborn is a naughty toddler now,
Mama is a full-time watchman now.
Laughter, tears, and each discovery;
Motherhood also is a real-time story.

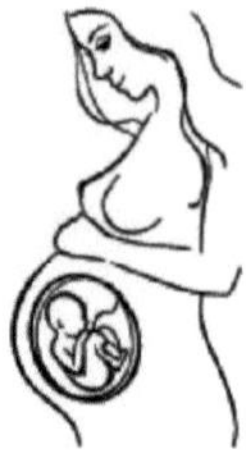

....

Shine of each other's diamond glow,
Inversely together they both grow.
Baby's first journey, mom's first baby;
First togetherness of sun and snow.

STRANGERS

I love strangers:
They don't know me,
I don't know myself,
We are so similar!

No claims,
No settlements,
Crossing paths,
Sharing smiles.

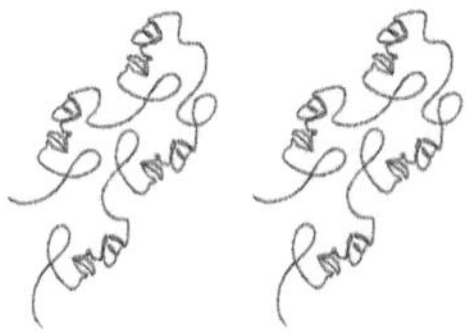

No small talk,
No pep talk,
Some silence,
Some anecdotes.

Are we like-minded?
What's our background?
We have nothing to do.
Nothing is programmed.

No past,
No future,
No carbon footprint,
Eco-friendly stories.

....

I love strangers!
They don’t know me,
I don’t know myself,
We are so similar.

....

DOT .

Push me, you will find it locked.
Pull me, you will find it heavy.
See through and you will see a reflection...

....
I am, who else, but a dot
amongst a zillion connecting dots…
Neither a stopping period
nor a stamping full stop.

I have no master,
I have no slave—
live in no mansion,
I live in no cave.

Come from the street,
I go to the street—
see you there darling,
down the street.

I am a drop,
I am the dust—
in me is you,
and I am in you.

How many streets
In this large earthy world?
How many 'I's and 'me's
In these streets of this world?
How many worlds
Orbiting that huge hot sun?
How many stars
In the fringes like the sun?
How many milky ways
In a bag of a billion such things?
How many such bagfuls
Make this universe of all things?
How many galaxies are then
In the universe, in our nature here?
How many more universes
Closed off somewhere greater there?

Infinite creations…
You and I—agents.
Not controllers, not originators—
mere dotting agents.

I am a drop,
I am the dust—
in me is you,
and I am in you.

………
I am, who else, but a dot
amongst a zillion connecting dots…
Neither a stopping period
nor a stamping full stop.
………

Why push and pull as creators?
Push me, you will find it locked.
Pull me, you will find it heavy.
See through and you will see a reflection…

………
I am, who else, but a dot
amongst a zillion connecting dots…
Neither a stopping period
nor a stamping full stop.
………

WHEN I LEFT ME

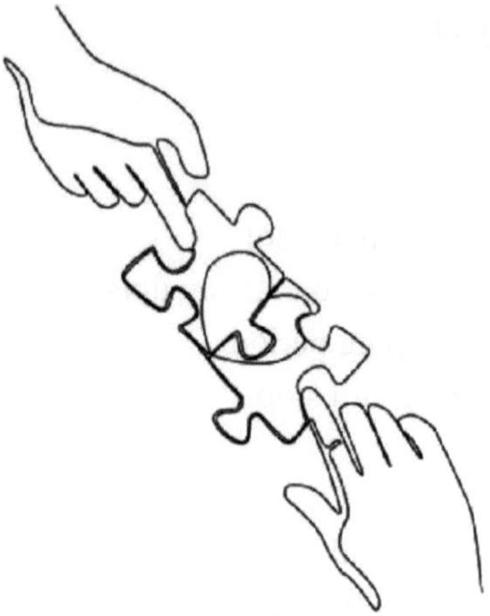

When ‘I’ left ‘me’,
‘I’ and ‘me’ separated to become two.
Factors multiplied freely
Created boundless multiples of two.
‘I’ is now free from ‘me’
I am now free from me
I and me are both now free
Nearing the elegance of ‘we’.

To be ‘we’, is to be you and I;
To be ‘we’, is not to be me and I.

WE

‘I’ is a highway
‘U’ is a turning point
‘We’—the odyssey

TWIN SOULS

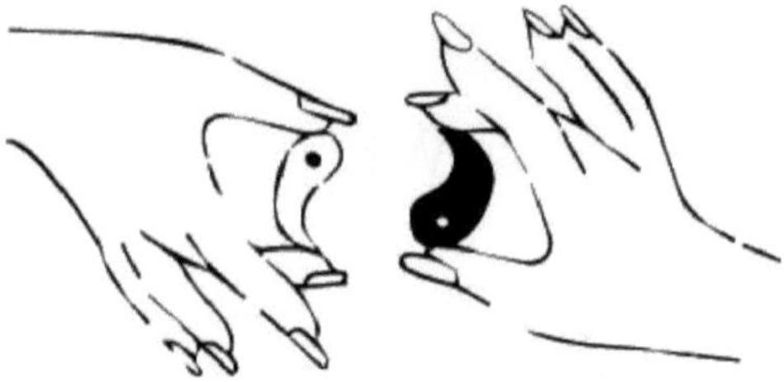

One for love,
The other for truth.
One for living,
The other for reflecting.
One for seeking,
The other for giving.
One for health,
The other for the soul.
One for happiness,
The other for bliss.
One for the good times,
The other for service.
One for fun and play,
The other for care and share.
One for the small moments,
The other for timelessness.
One for life,
Both for life.
One keeps the other,
The other keeps the one.

THIRSTY WATER

A wave runs over sand
Thirsty water drinking land.

Stones unable to swim
Wished they were softer!
Prayers graciously taken
In a gulp by the thirsty water…

BEING ALIVE

Smile of a stranger,
Small gaze of a lover,
A cat contentedly purring,
A dog playfully barking.

An imperfect homely little room,
Flowers that beautifully bloom,
Food made with love and care,
Moments that we freely share.

Baking scent traveling in the air,
Wind feeling your face and hair,
Laughter coming from children at play,
Thought of a cup of tea on a rainy day.

In the quiet moments, soft and slow;
When ideas strike, understandings grow—
Gentle murmur like a river gliding inside…
Do I need eyes to witness the sky outside?

Birdsong breaking the hush of night,
Brand new day to make things right,
The simple act of being alive—
Where else does happiness thrive?

WATCH TIME

A better looking watch
does not guarantee better times ahead;
Better times however bring
many a better looking watch, true that.

THEY WOULD COME BACK

They said,
they would come back—
they would come back to us
one day as people's guilt!

Ubiquitous roadside trees
came to me one day
on one of my long drives.
Bigger wider roads,
faster fancier cars,
trees became invisible scars.

The childhood river
came to me one day
in a child's wall painting.
Machines, AI, factories,
people smarter than yore,
the river was no more.

Hearts that we fell for
came to me one day
as a bluesy night-song.
Cyberspace, cloud, Wi-Fi,
no more as blue is the sky,
hearts feeling shamelessly shy.
………
They said,
they would come back—
they would come back to us
one day as people's guilt!
………

R.E.D.

Work hard.
Keep on keeping on.
Discipline, consistency, persistence—
Revolve.
....

Search for meanings.
Discover a mirror, ask questions.
Get better, improve with time—
Evolve.
....

Keep reinventing.
Break yourself, design yourself.
Be metaphysical, be a nobody—
Dissolve.
....

MANIFESTO

When strength looks into the mirror
it beholds vulnerability.
And vice versa.

Frictions between
fractions of a human being—
such ordinary
yet
wonderfully significant stories
of our being.

Do not ever
hide anything
about you
from yourself.
Would you wait for the miracles of time
to gift you a dream life?
Or, do you wish to be a child,
running bare feet, unprotected from aliens,
searching for your fertile oasis?

....
Truth does not lie
unless
it is a mere sound effect
to please the ears.
....
Who has a watch as finely made
that showed moments but times?
Who has palms as large to carry along
the footsteps, evenings, and sweet chimes?

Life shall love you tenderly at times.
Life shall burn you to ashes at times.
Would you
stop your engine
and keep honking
at your manifested life?
Would you wait
for miracles and blessings
to be poured on your head?
Or, would you be that child
born to be free and wisely wild?

‘YOUR YOU’ : ‘THEIR YOU’

People—we meet along—
multitude of them—
do not wish to stay.
Not designed to stay.

Mountains to climb, ladders to build;
Bridges to connect, paths to find;
Oceans to drink, fires to meet;
Anchors to draw, changes to greet;
Some have excuses, some have doubts;
Some have clarity layered with some clouds.

It’s not that they don’t stay,
stay they do, they do stay.
However, stay they with ‘their you’,
stay they don’t with ‘your you’.

Your version of you
which you trust and call ‘your you’,
meets their version of you
that they brand and call ‘their you’.

‘Your you’ is changing, perpetually evolving.
Why do you then pull in others to be staying?
Let them move with ‘their you’,
as you keep moving with ‘your you’.

SERIOUS FUN

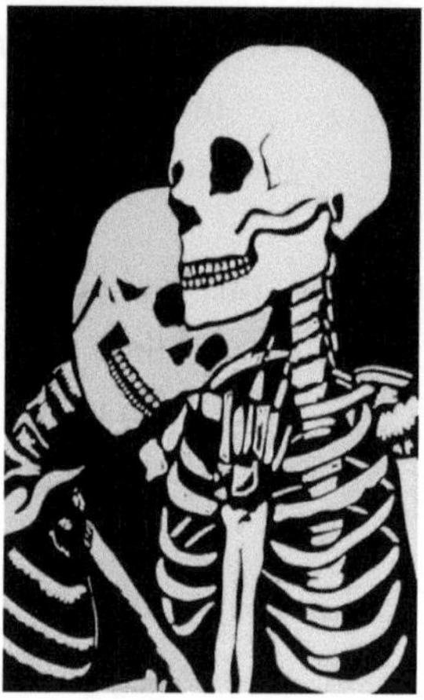

And I meet people
taking their own selves
so very seriously,
that they would not know
that they would not
leave this world alive;
that they would not know
purposefully driven men
and most intense women
are all having fun
breaking their own selves
till they are alive!

HAVE YOU BEEN?

"The world is a strange place," people say.
"Compared to which place?" I ask.
"Have you been to some place else?"
....

INFINITY

She wanted to sing.
Waited for the skies to sing along.
Then she met her alter ego,
singing solo a tiny mirror song:
“All that jazz and highs
You don’t need the skies
It’s on you and no one else to be
To be your core chorus!
So, be your own chorus!
Your own chorus!”

She wrote her first verse that night,
daring to be her own chorus:
………

How far we traversc
Is our search for us
Countering the adverse
We are the core chorus
Limitless possibilities
Taking own shapes
Unlocking an odyssey
Whatever it takes…
No more do I see a limited sky outside,
As infinity flies in my unlimited inside.
No more do I see a limited sky outside,
As infinity flies in my unlimited inside.

WHAT'S IN THE MIDDLE

Bread is tasty
on both sides,
but,
what’s in the middle—
what makes the middle—
makes
or
breaks
a sandwich.

....

Between
looking back
and
looking ahead,
just don’t let
today slip by!

....

A bite of the sandwich
and your soul realizes
how much love
has gone into its making.
How both sides
have held with love
the messy but tasty middle—
multiplying manyfolds
its love for feeding.

....

A walk across moments today
and your soul realizes—
with all heart and much love
why yesterday and tomorrow
brought you to the middle today,
such dearly telling you to live every day,
bringing you wrapped in disguises
every day's beautiful gift of 'today'!

....

UNSEEN-UNBEEN

If all wishes were granted
(then) there would be no art.

Imagine all the places you have been to
and you shall find them in your heart.
Imagine all the places you have not been to
and you shall find them in your dreams.
That's the beauty of creativity,
the pricelessness of art!

Don't need time and money
to build hearts and dreams.
Eternities could be built
from unseen-unbeen realms.

ONCE A HEAVY SHOWER

Once a heavy shower
said to a tiny droplet of water,
“Go away, I don’t need you anymore.”

The droplet waited and waited.
Tried hard to stay.
But it had to leave.

Soon the shower became crazier.
And then thinner. And weaker.
Finally, the sun ate it up.

UMBRELLA STORIES

Summer days
Gardens everywhere
Flowers blooming
Umbrellas blooming
Tough to say
Which is what.

Morning school
Pouring heavily
Bus conductor
Walking kids
Single umbrella
One by one.

Young woman
Riding scooty
Taking a walk
Ditching her scooty
Raincoat is bore
Umbrella is love.

College times
Canteen coffee
Droplets dripping
Anxious body
Hoping for rain
Dry umbrella.

Black and white
Old feature film
Raining romance
Singing melody
Two bodies
One umbrella.

Public bus
Co-passengers
Breaking the ice
Talking umbrellas
Nice design
Where from.

Railway station
Heartland India
Hanging umbrellas
Busy compartments
Kept for the last mile
Without conveyance.

Fruit market
Lady vendor
Offering shade
Beating heat
Fruit smoothie
Under an umbrella.

Old man
Eighty years
Old black umbrella
Fifty years
All weather
Everyday friend.

Dak bungalow
Carpet lawn
Morning tea
Newspapers
Large umbrella
Rainbow coloured.

Storeroom
In backyard
Spider web
Dusty scent
Broken umbrella
Woken nostalgia.

"Roof in rain
Shade from sun
Miss me not!
I am the one!"
Embroidery of love
Etched on my umbrella.

RAIN LOVERS

Have you seen rain lovers
Who wake up with the clouds
Open their doors, break ceilings
Drench their bodies, worries, feelings
Drizzle, spray or pour; always go to work
Nothing can distract, service does not stop
Livelihood must come, must run the home
Burdens to uphold, work does not stop.

Have you seen rain lovers
Who invite home the clouds,
Open their windows, sit on the balcony;
Connect with nature to find a euphony…
Poets of beauty, artists of the world;
Painting and singing a romantic world…
Pitter-patter on the roof,
racing rate of heart…
Making love with dear ones
rain lovers and art.

Have you seen the third kind—
Rain lovers like you, I, and us—
On a car wheel,
or wary of mud-splashing car wheels.
Carelessly splashing,
or carefully maneuvering their wheels.
Walking carefully from puddles on the streets,
or walking joyfully there itself.
Protecting hair, shoes, clothes to be in order,
or making paper boats with shoes themselves.
Romantics at heart,
with daily obligations to cover.
Sitting in a cubicle or someplace else,
with the eyes of a forlorn lover.
Forgotten raincoats in small tea shops…
smells of sweat and rain at city bus stops…
Mixture of the first two is the third—
bit of one, a bit of type two is the third.

Then, there are rain lovers so hard—
Facing the music while clouds rock hard!
Thin windows, ceiling down to their floors;
How to survive, anaemic are their doors!
Flooded households, hopes and fears;
Inundated by water but invisible tears!
Prayers and desperations this too shall pass,
Only a few pull through, not everyone does!

FROG IN MY SHOES

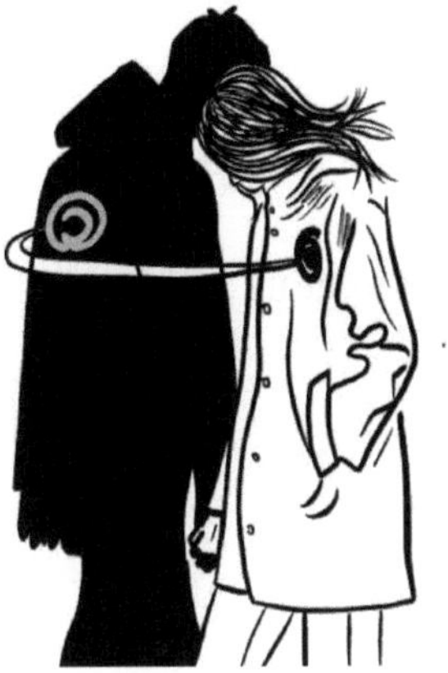

Nobody understands
fully wholly
despite wholehearted efforts
anybody else.

We live
with interpretations convenient,
with feelings of not being understood,
with feelings of not being able to understand.

We might as well
prefer to not be understood.
As such put up a front,
as if we don't care.

A middle path
is to make claims
of smiles and tears,
anger or indifference.
I understand you
but you do not.
So much effort I put in
but you do not.

As if bargaining a deal,
wittingly or unwittingly.
And then another path,
albeit not a flowery one,
is to feel and know
understanding is humane.
A practice trippy abstract
better left wide open.

There is a frog
living in a pair of my shoes.
I wear them daily
they are not my old shoes.
When I wear them
the frog is not to be found,
When I store them
the frog makes it a home.
Such is understanding and its ambiguity…
Touchwood!

Ambiguous layers of every life:
Are we humans any different?
Or, do we seek to be understood,
but, do not want to understand?

....

The shift
from sympathy to empathy—
a mighty thin line—very fragile.
Handle with care please.
Respect that.

....

BEST COULD HAVE BEEN

To be understood by a fellow being
beyond a stretch of time
and a series of situations
is like the best poem
a poet has never written
or the best painting
an artist has not yet painted
or the best song unsung, unheard
or the best film not imagined, not filmed
or the best dream
that did not come to the eyes
or the best miracle
that fell shy of taking place
or a relationship
or tomorrow
or a world—
all the best things that could have been!

8PM: 8AM

8 PM:
when promises are made
entrepreneurs are born
selves identify as artists
revolutionaries realize the purpose of life
visionaries suddenly sense their third eye
good vibes hang out with brotherhood
and changing the tides of times
is just a matter of time now dude.

8 AM:
when people are fast asleep,
or, too busy to wonder about
anything else than what's on hand,
or, focused and fixated on a routine,
or, maybe, sober and wise once again,
identifying with needs, wants, and more;
realizing oneself and justifying to others—
maintaining the status quo is a painful fine art.

………
Twelve hours are enough for the truth.
Rest, good or poor jokes, as per your taste.
………

RETROSPECTION

Retrospection is a bitch.
Go back on a trip,
feel all possible emotions,
and when you come back to today,
you realize—
you have lost so many friends,
a range of quality virtues,
a bunch of hair,
maybe a couple of teeth,
and instead gained—
some age without grace,
a little knowledge without wisdom,
a lot of misconceptions,
a few wrinkles,
and kilos of fleshy weight.

I love that bitch.
I love retrospection.
It is an introspection on rewind mode.
A bitchy true rewind mode.

PHOTOGRAPHS

Turning the pages
from black and white
to being close to colours
to being saturated colours.
Clicking buttons
Scrolling screens
Who is who
Beyond recognition!

Mind runs…
Eyes shut.
What do you see?
Anonymous faces alongside mine?
People who never knew
they walked together.
Never being told
they captured inner rooms.

A blur of faces
and behind them
a bokeh of blurry eyes.
Pursuit of a touch.
Comfort of a taste.
A collage of sensations.
Some known places.
Some known colours.
Fashions and hairstyles.
A smell, many smells.
Casting a nano spell.
Gone in seconds.

Voices speaking.
Whispering, shouting.
Voices silent. Speaking in silence.
Living parallel lives that will never really meet.
Unfurling traces of own selves forever discreet.

A flash of white.
A streak of red.
Eyes closed.
What do you see?
Photographs captured in the mind:
Hiding and seeking as they please.

INVISIBLE EYEGLASSES

How long do you need, a day or years?
How long would you sing in your own ears?
Wearing each other's invisible eyeglasses,
are secrets fooling around in joys and tears?

Is it a flaw that I can see you
without really ever seeing you?
Isn't it magical what you gave me
through the spaces created for me?

A piece of heart taking a detour
or, a seeking bird losing its way?
We are straight lines running crooked
so much yet so very little to say.

Returning home for the day
I can sense an ocean and you…
It won't take me much long
to wear a shirt and smile like you.

People who do not want anything
aren't they the ones that feel everything?
People who have never felt your skin
don't they still secretly smell in your skin?

OBJECTS IN THE MIRROR

A fast car out on its voyage—
Rearview mirrors running like a movie,
Faces and places whisper in my ears,
Lessons and laughter oh-so groovy.

Smelling through visuals—
An old road from light years far,
Listening to your smile in a picture,
What is still is moving itself like a fast car.

Time is a naughty hipster—
Chasing us dearly to remind…
Echoes of what has been,
What we thought we left behind.

What is crossing you—
What just went past you—
Nothing, my friend,
is as far as they seem to appear;
Objects in the mirror
are much closer than they appear.

Images take you inside,
Reflections bring day to night,
Butterflies back in the tummy,
Hope is no more out of sight...

Timelines, symbols, truth:
What all have you seen?
Nothing is far from the truth—
Not as far as seemed to be seen.

Speed of mind won't stop…
Spirit of youth would know for good…
Why leave behind what you can take?
If only we felt we would!

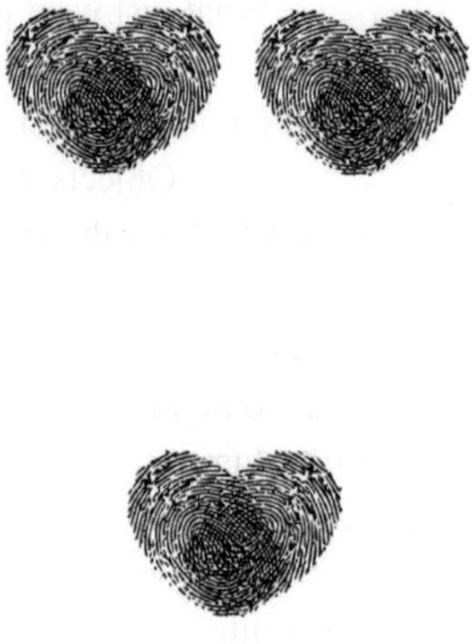

LITTLE THINGS

Touching hearts
is as easy
as being touched!
So easy
that it still
has no formula.

The little things
do a little bigger
than bigger things.
Be naturally little.
It's okay being a little sweet.
Just don't sugarcoat though.
Don't give others a cavity…
Who says you lack gravity?!

Glaze of shining stars,
We are all dots of stardust.
Little things as we are,
Keep at it, keeping the trust.

SHORT STORY

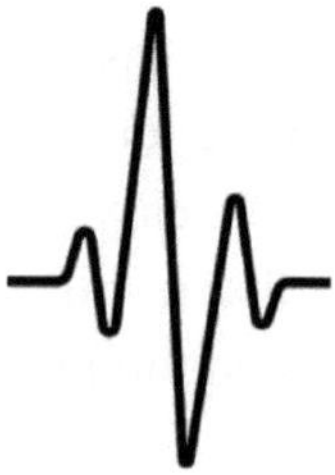

He did not utter.
She did not listen.

She did not gaze.
He did not behold.

Some love stories are as short.

LONG STORY

He did not utter.
She heard a lovesong.

She did not gaze.
He saw oceans and skies.

Some love stories are as long.

YOU BE IT

If not the rains
Clouds be it.
If not the garden
A rose be it.
If not the roads
Few steps be it.
If not the time yet
Some wine be it.
If not the skies
A smile be it.
If not the oceans
A gaze be it.
If not the fire
An embrace be it.
If not much air
You, love, be it!

HOW I WISH!

A lone cat's night walk
A hanging creaking bridge
A full moon's naked face atop a hill
A row of adolescent waltzing trees
A horse couple's neigh
A cool valley breeze
A passing stream singing to me all night
"Go gentle on the curves, my sweets…"

How I wish you were here!
How I wish it dear!

SENDING SKIES…

Alien wanderer friend,
What name do I call you by?
My heart feels for you…
In the canvas of the drunk sky!

Hey, the sky shall sleep
Amidst our ripe paddy fields
Cool breeze, tranquil night
Shyness is breaking shields
May flowers bloom
Melting every ice
Two wishes breathe
Distance is the spice

We meet on the clouds,
Cloud number nine.
As you send me your sky
And I send you mine…

MARK THE DATES

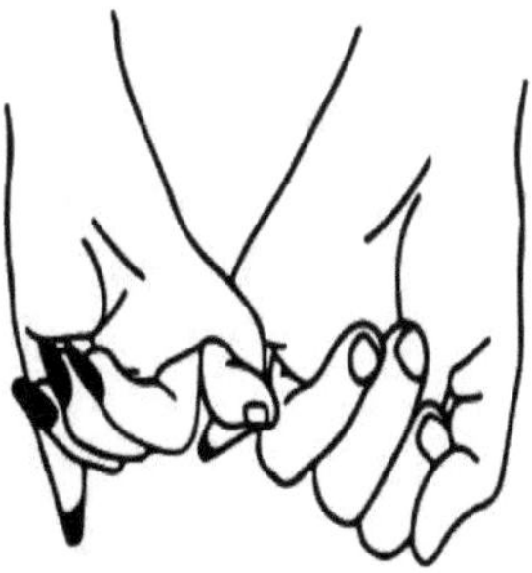

Her January Eyes
His February Voice
Her March Smile
His April Bouquet
Her May Fragrance
His June Charm
Her July Blush
His August Hope
Her September Coffee
His October Touch
Her November Night
His December Dream

TO BE CONTINUED…

“In the garden of evening mist;
the air that brings you back to life,
the air that you say goes unnoticed,
isn’t that nothing but me?
So very lucky you are,”
she said.

“In the bed of days and nights;
the pillow that embraces you,
the pillow that is otherwise mundane,
isn’t that nothing but me?
Unbelievably lucky you are,”
he retorted.

Sweet nothings
Sharp banters
Airy thoughts
Pillow fights
Household chores
To be continued…

WHY WRITE?

Why write
the already written?

Flower and bird
—silently—
exchanged their feelings
with a question.

Why write
the already written?

TAKE ME HOME

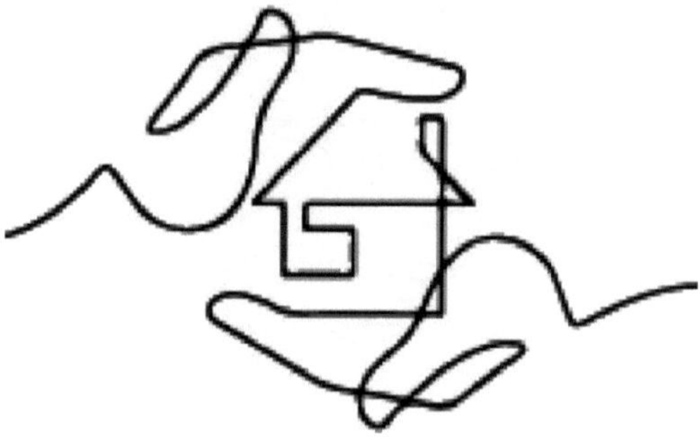

On a roadside stall in a hut,
a flower vase caught the self's eyes.

It said,
"Take me home."
The self refused,
"But I don't have flowers."
It countered,
"Take me home as an excuse—
as an excuse to create a garden."

The vase walked home with the self.
A garden blossomed in their yard.
Flowers—by the names of
magic,
charm,
haunting,
and, wit—
are blooming there lovingly
painting their lives
all four seasons.

SELF, YOUNGER SELF

One night on a highway
the self met its younger self
and caught up.

Self:	How come you are here, Sonny?
Younger Self:	I thought I'd ask you that, Oldie!
Self:	These are our ways. I thought your age and generation won't bother much about these ways.
Younger Self:	No. I come here often. Some of my friends frequent too.
Self:	Okay. Is it so? And how goes life?
Younger Self:	Going alright. Having fun. And you?

Self: It's fine.
Chilling
and going through motions.
Balancing both.

Younger Self: Then tell me about balance.
How do I find balance in life?

Self: In which aspect of life?

Younger Self: I don't know about aspects.
Just that I want this phase of life
to get over soon.
I want to earn my own money
and be independent.
Tell me how did you do it?

Self: I also used to think
like this at your age.
But trust me,
when you would be my age,
you would yearn to be going back
to this phase of your life.

Younger Self: Really?

Self: Yes.

Younger Self: Why so?

Self: Because you never find
balance in life.
It's just an illusion.

Younger Self: But you said
you are balancing life?

Self:	Correct and incorrect both.
Younger Self:	What do you mean? You are contradicting yourself.
Self:	You are right. We are devices of contradictions.
Younger Self:	But why did you say you were balancing?
Self:	I never said I have found the balance. I said I am balancing… Meaning, trying to balance… Learning everyday… Trying to learn.
Younger Self:	How do you chill then? Where is the fun?
Self:	You sound so much like my younger self! Rebellious, argumentative, and so very difficult to talk to. Zero in listening skills.
Younger Self:	But you don't sound at all like the older self I want to grow up to be. Zero in flair and style. A self-contradicting man. And why are you so verbose?

Self:	Have fun then…Bye.
Younger Self:	Okay. Learn balancing then…

On another night on another highway
the self met its younger self.
They both have gained a bit—
age, weight, and listening skills.
They shared a drink that night.
Spoke more in silence.
Received before transmitting.
Their gap shrank miraculously—
Sonny: less edgy, more engaging, calmer.
Oldie: less verbose, free spirited, younger.

TRUE LOVE

People's interest in you
turn into—
bonhomie,
fondness,
like,
lust,
habit,
dependence,
indifference,
disinterest,
and sometimes
go to the extremes
of love and hate.

Amidst all these, what is true love?
I don't know any untrue love.

WISDOM'S DOOM

You love red
Go after violet
And complain about
Not finding yellow.
....

Wisdom says minimalism:
Focus on your needs.
Smartphones and algorithms
Merging wants and needs.

Wisdom says control:
Know your limits.
Credit cards laughing—
Are there any limits?

Wisdom says meditate:
Don't get distracted.
Parties, late nights, inboxes—
Focused. Dedicated.

Wisdom says travel and eat:
Why post on FBs and Instagrams?
Vanity says memories they are;
Belongingness with holograms.

Wisdom says solitude is gold:
Brings you closer to yourself.
FOMO says find the best angle;
Don't miss a picture of yourself.

Wisdom says learn to commit:
Don't leave love searching for a lover.
Choices and chances agree to disagree—
Convenient being a confused lover.

....
You love red
Go after violet
And complain about
Not finding yellow.
....

MONEY DUDE

When you need money
Dude is your dude,
When he lends money
Dude is buddy good.
When you don't pay back
Dude gets no text, no call;
Till he doesn't ask it back
Dude gets no courtesy call.

When dude asks it back
Excuses are made,
Funny stories and
More excuses are made.
Deadlines pass in vain
Silence is tightly kept,
Until dude asks again
Status quo is kept.

One day you drift away
Without any fight,
Run out of what to say
Inside you is the fight.
Dude is no longer a dude
Just a random friend,
No closeness between you
Just a normal trend!

Even you yourself know
So much that you lied,
Don't say that you don't know
That you hardly tried.
Parties, trips, showoffs
Did not cut down much,
Took for granted your dude
Knowing he won't ask much.

Problems that you face
We do empathize with,
Problems that dude has
You don't empathize with.

Dude has a garden at home
with a thousand trees,
Money plants with real money
are creeping on those trees!

EMPTY WALLET

The young boy
with dark sun-dried skin,
thin body, hungry stomach,
but diamond-bright eyes—
kept an empty wallet in his pocket.
He collected garbage disposals.

The self asked one day,
“How much money do you keep
in the close-to-heart wallet that you keep?”
With a broad smile, the boy said,
“No money, Sir!”

Amused as well as bemused,
the self asked again,
“Why do you always carry it then—
so close to your heart, on your chest?”

Once again replied the young boy
with bright-diamond eyes
and a pearl-white smile,
“This is a reminder to myself, Sir!
This is what I have to change, Sir!
One day I’ll change the status quo
and have money in my wallet, Sir!”

WHAT IS BECAUSE WHAT IS NOT

Sunlight sunset
What is because what is not?
White, black, or grey
Where is light, where is not?

Binary opposites of joy and grief
Laughter and tears, lengthy and brief
Now and gone, presence and absence
Yes and no, sensible and nonsense

Your day is someone's night
Your dull is someone's bright
Fixed objectivity, fluid subjectivity
Matters of time, coupled with sensitivity…

Or, nothing is because nothing is not?
Spinning my head, cause spinning I am not?
Tossing of a coin, two sides to the spin;
One leads to a loss, the other to a win.
As you ask the coin for secrets to glory,
Two sides smile to take you to a story.
Nothing is forever, fate does not stay,
Keeps moving places, every night and day.
....
They, who, keep the courage;
do not kill the hope;
Fate mostly hangs out with them
with a longer rope.
But, it does not mean
it would always work;
However, it means
that it might just work.
You lose some, you find some;
running cold and hot;
Something came to you cause
something has come not.
....
....
Sunlight sunset
What is because what is not?
White, black, or grey
Where is light, where is not?
....

LONE STAR

As I asked a lone star one night:
"What is the heaviest of all?"

It blinked one twinkle little time to say:
"An empty heart!"

THIN LINES

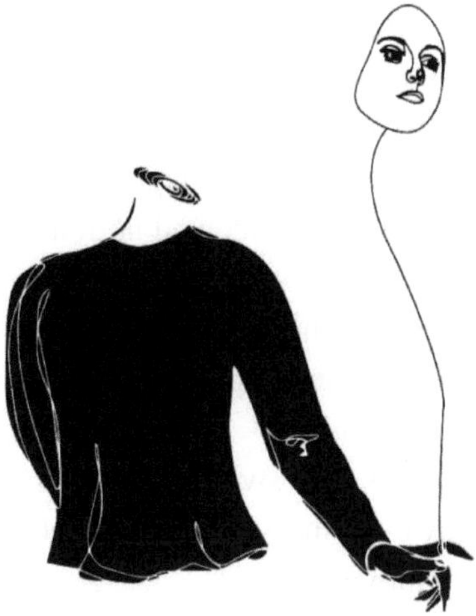

The lines are thin, my friends. Very thin.
A gift is a curse at times.
Thinking and overthinking.
Sensitivity and hypersensitivity.

There are no gymnasiums for mental health.
No one can sweat it out with you.
No one may talk to you about that as well.
Because, once again,
the line
between empathy and sympathy
is thin, my friends.
Very very thin.

How about being
a piece of sponge that absorbs pain?
Or, must we be
walls bouncing back thoughts and feelings?
Do we ever know,
who we just might have caused more pain
with our preconceived notions?

Intellect can be an ego.
Feelings can be perceived to be overrated.
Soul searching
takes its own sweet and sour time.
However, in its imperfect flight,
life moves on,
the engine being health—
physical, mental, emotional,
spiritual, holistic, and the like…

Talking and sharing can help the cause,
experts say.
How about learning to keep secrets of others?
Or, must we break anyone's trust
by sharing their secrets that they shared with us?

How about gossiping less?
Or, must we gossip at all?
Strong people do not care about gossip.
Not everyone is as strong as you are though.

How about accepting
different people as different people?
Or, must we brand
and tag them as strange peculiar people?

What about body shaming?
What about mind shaming?
What about thoughts shaming?
What about feelings shaming?

We can help only with empathy, my friends.
Neither by indifference, nor by sympathy.
Do love unconditionally.
Do not take relationships for granted as patterns.
Do not exploit anyone's work and talent.
Value contributions.
Respect.
Period.

How about we being healthy ourselves?
How else but by introspection?
How else but by being true to ourselves?
And if needed,
by seeing a doctor,
an expert, a specialist;
one who has
technical understanding of these things.

People say, be your best friend.
How about being a good friend first—
to you and to others?
We all need that one friend.

The universe will conspire to connect you
to that one special friend—
could be in the shape of a friend per se,
a brother, a sister, a father, a mother,
a relative, a lover, a husband, a wife,
a girlfriend, a boyfriend,
a teacher, a mentor,
a colleague, a senior, a junior,
an acquaintance,
an online friendship,
or even a stranger at times…

INSIDERS : OUTSIDERS

Everywhere you go
Always there would be
Some insiders
And some outsiders.

Insiders getting all the favours
Outsiders hardly getting their due
Narrow-minded being an approach
Human race loses out on itself—
Talent, service, productivity,
Culture and evolution eventually.

Case is,
on which side are you?
Which side of the coin are you?

There are insiders—
cause they belong somewhere
by birth
or background
or by chance
or by design
or through validation
—bona fide insiders who belong somewhere.

There are outsiders
cause they don't belong anywhere.
But no more remain they outsiders
as once they start belonging somewhere.

Case is,
on which side are you?
Which side of the coin are you?
The feelings, that of being an outsider,
do you still feel now that you are an insider?

Humankind is designed to feel
a sense of belonging—
to serpentine spirals—
that bind us as insiders
and divide us from outsiders:
where do you come from,
which school that you went to,
which language that you speak,
what really drives you passionately,

how compromised are your values,
how do you enjoy spending your time,
your economics, politics, aesthetics;
culture, comfort, convenience;
and likewise,
and likewise.
Your circle and your centre
may not always be able to
empathize with one another though.

Working hard to fit in—
Chilling out together,
Spreading good vibes,
Keeping the spirits high,
Commenting 'awesome' on mediocre work,
Belonging to a lobby, gang, or camp,
Boosting the ego like an alter ego.
Your circle and your centre
may not always be able to
empathize with one another though.

Seeking insiders' validation…
Yearning for belongingness…
Need versus wants…
Mind over matter…

You have faced that;
or, you have not.
You will face that;
or, you will not.
You have made someone feel that;
or, you have not.
You will make someone feel that;
or, you will not.
Case is,
on which side are you?
Which side of the coin are you?

………

Everywhere you go
Always there would be
Some insiders
And some outsiders.

………

EMPTY CHAIR EP: 1

Mentor texted Mentee
Picture of a chair empty
Asking a question—
"What makes of it your intuition?"

"If everyone kept an empty chair
everyone else would have a place to sit."
Replied Mentee.

Mentor texted back with a smiley—
"Beautiful!
Most beautiful thing
I have heard
in quite a long time!"

EMPTY CHAIR EP: 2

Mentee asked Mentor—
"What is humility?"
Mentor replied—
"Humility is reading reality."
Mentee flexed in confusion his eyebrows.

Mentor texted Mentee
Picture of a chair empty.
Same as before. A chair empty,
and a question—
"What makes of it your intuition?"

"But I already answered that, Sir!"
Mentee exclaimed.
"That was beautiful!"
Mentor responded.
"What you said the other day,
that was really beautiful!
Now, what is the truth of this picture?
What is the truth beyond the beauties?"

Mentee shrugged his shoulders.
Paused in bewilderment.
Before he could text back,
in no time came the reply on its own—
as if it was always written there—
just not seen,
just not read before.

Mentor: "Someone sat here,
and someone will sit here.
The seat is occupied
only temporarily.
Permanence
of a changing seat
is its recurring emptiness.
Knowing that is humility.
Knowing that is reading reality.
....
....

We are here, one by one,
to keep passing the baton.
Who else are we?!
What else are we for?!"

ANCHOR POINTS EP: 1

Awed by the imageries,
conversations, feelings, queries;
as the self pinched the self,
the self realized this was not a dream.

....

"Which one of the tires is punctured?"
Asked a lady's voice,
invisible body and face,
introducing herself as the guardian of the jungle.

"The stepney is punctured, the rest are fine."
As the self replied,
the lady's voice burst into a laughter
and said, "Why are you waiting then?"

"Because the stepney may be required.
There may be tougher terrains ahead."
The self went ahead in conversation,
"And I am lost as well!"

A soft warm hand, still invisible,
that the self could feel,
handed over a stick of chalk,
walked a few miles holding hands…

"What do you do when you feel lost?"
—the invisible lady's voice asked
and pushed the self further into the jungle.
It was dense. It became denser.

As the self got anxious and felt further lost,
the lady's voice ate the moon and stars
and vanished saying,
"Find yourself, when you are lost."
It was dark, it became darker…

ANCHOR POINTS EP: 2

Wanderer self's vision was blurry
as it was dense, smoky and foggy;
no curves or bends could be seen—
flames of a leaping fire could only be seen.

As the self did behold
a moth moving to the fire—
without a push
the self too moved towards the fire.

Soon, the fire disappeared.
The moth went with the fire.
It became pitch dark once again.
in that darkness,
a tree came into the self's vision.

The stick of chalk,
that an invisible lady had previously handed,
pulled the self's hands
and walked up with him to the tree.
The self marked a heart on the tree.
The lady's voice returned briefly,
"You travel with your anchor points hereon…"
And vanished once again.

As the self pinched the self,
the self realized this was not a dream.
Another tree came into vision,
and then another, one after the other—
marking hearts with the magic chalk,
drawing anchor points one after the other…

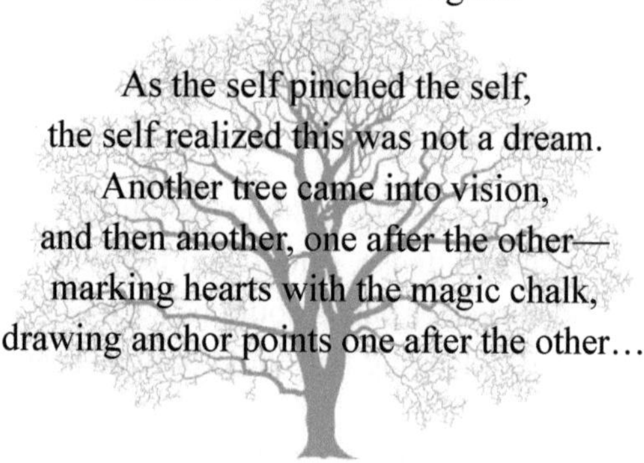

EMBRACING EVOLVING

Turning two mistakes
into three fruitful lessons,
Making two heartbreaks
into three glorious stories,
Forgetting two habit patterns
to make three new habits,
Forgiving two toxic friends
to make three golden allies,
Accepting two hard failures
to get set go three more times…

Turn your multiplicity of two into three.
You are many.
And more.
And more.
Two and three don't add to be five,
Two and three multiply to be six.

MISTAKES

Time: “Why do you
keep making so many mistakes?”

Moments: “So that you feel good pointing out.
....
Had I not made those mistakes,
I would not be called moments.
....
And frankly dear,
how would time have so much fun
if mistakes are removed from it?”

Time: “True that…
How would time have fun
if moments don’t live in it!”

I DIDN'T

I didn't light the lamp
We—the lamp and I—wished it to be lit
The night was a witness.

I didn't mould the goblet
We—the clay and I—gave it a shape
The clay-wheel supported us.

I didn't lay the garden
We—the flowers and I—
picked colours and fragrances…
The sun and the rains took very good care.

EXCHANGING BREATHS

Season of the fall,
leaves starting to fall…
Uninhabited till far
mankind went into a shell, wrapping a shawl.

A wanderer, bereft of company,
stopped by a tree, leaves fell on him.
Frail feather light leaves
falling heavily on him.

"Hey you, what brings you here?"
—a voice resonated there…
Feeling awkward in the chest
the wanderer felt a bit heavy there…

From the bouquet of leaves pouring
one tiny leaf walked up to him—
mixing innocence and inquisitiveness
asked tiny little tough things to him.

"Mankind of spring, are you one too?
Why do you all leave in the fall?
Flimsy light leaves feel heavy with grief;
What is now, tell me, the heaviest of all?"

Wanderer pitched a tent, ditched the roof;
Shedding tree shook her leg merrily.
Together, they gazed at the button-like stars,
Exchanging breaths, existing blissfully!

EXTINCT QUESTIONS

From
extinct birds
and
animals
to
entire flora and fauna
and then
extinct humankind,
....
As two friends sat down to drink—
one asked the other—
"What does extinct humankind mean?
Does it mean kindness in humans is no more?
Or, does it mean
a specific class of humans is no more?
Don't they make it like them anymore?"

The other friend thought
and then he thought
and then he poured another drink.
"Have they changed so drastically?
Or, have they evolved emotionally
to survive into being another creature?
Or, have they mysteriously vanished
to another planet?"—he asked this time.

They poured more drinks…
Evening became midnight.
Then it became morning.

What they saw
waking up in the morning,
they don't remember
how did this happen!
Written on the room wall
in bold—

SURVIVAL TO CULTURE
OR, CULTURE TO SURVIVAL?
SURVIVAL IS THE CULTURE
OR, CULTURE IS THE SURVIVAL?

GOOD MORNING!

The window to his east became brighter…
Welcomed the morning sun for light to enter.
An old stagnant ceiling fan
caught his morning eyes.
"Needs some cleaning,"
he thought, rubbing his eyes.

It's a humid hot May morning,
feeling hotter, due to routine load shedding.
As if he slept sound all night with AC on,
our man is strikingly fresh-looking.

Said a little gratitude
and got out of his bed.
Cell phone rang on nearby table,
but he did not check.
Started making the unkempt bed,
stretching his shoulders and neck.

"Everything else can wait.
Let me open the window,
behold the morning
and welcome it home.
Meet Mother Nature
and embrace what she holds.
Everything else can wait."
—he said inside him.

As he opened the window to his east,
in came a mild fan of cool breeze.
Verdant green it was that he saw,
showing teasers of a green day to seize.

A kitten jumped inside from the window,
made itself comfortable
on the newly made bed.
Our man smiled looking at.

A dog barked outside a door to his west
and pushed the door open
as the master said, "Come in, Sir!"
Big dog entered,
jumped onto the bed,
took the kitten in its embrace,
they both quickly fell asleep.
Nonchalant as they are!

Our man now went
towards his cell phone
to check who had called.
He said good morning loudly
while walking these few steps.
Nonchalant as he is!

G O O D M O R N I N G !

FEEDING<TRUSTING

"Isn't feeding a great deed?"
—asked a young vibrant girl, her mum.
As a herd of sheep grazed on her offerings.

"It's a joy, my dear."
Replied the mum to her daughter,
"Feeding is a joy.
Maybe, a great joy.
To some, the greatest joy."

Eager daughter more eager now,
"Why do people say
feeding is a great deed then?"

"Trust is a great deed,
not feeding alone.
You try to feed,
one accepts to be fed.
There lies a bond of trust."
Mother said,
putting her arm over her daughter's shoulders.

Eager daughter, repeating her eager question,
"Why do people say
feeding is a great deed then?"

Mother replied with a smile,
"It is, no doubt, a sacred job;
but people are too attached
and consumed by what they do.
They seek validation—
from others, or at least from the self.
When I feed someone
and consider that a great deed,
I am unwittingly belittling the ones who I feed;
and I ruin the sanctity of the job."

There was silence for a few seconds.
Mum continues breaking it,
"Instead, if I find joy in it—
in that bond of trust—
without seeking validation
of it being a great deed—
from others and from the self—
then, I just am extending my gratefulness
to be a factor in that trust."

"Mom, I am a young girl!"
The daughter cut her mother short,
"I am a young girl of flesh and blood,
I have worldly aspirations and inspirations.
What all are you teaching me?
Do you think I can comprehend all these?"

Mom kissed her girl's forehead,
"It's all about trust, my dear!
I am telling you in trust,
that you can feel the feeling.
Just look at the sheep you are feeding—
they are making us feel good; aren't they?
It's about a two-way trust, two-way joy;
We are humane, forever in search of little joy."

As the young girl looked at the sheep with love
and with happily moist eyes
looked at mum with love,
she murmured—
"And this feeling of joy,
truthfully,
does not care
about the degrees of greatness.
Why do we name it a great deed then?
Why else
but maybe
to entice people into doing it!
And keep doing it!"

....

Romanticizing
in the names of greatness and heroism
can attract most people.

Unassuming humaneness can attract,
sadly but realistically,
only a few humans, not many people.

....

CO-EXISTENTIAL

Mentor texted Mentee:
"One is never rich enough to buy art,
never poor enough to appreciate it.
—what do you make of it?"

Mentee replies a few moments hence:
"Money can buy the commodity of art,
not the mind of an artist;
poverty can stop from buying art,
not from appreciating an artist's mind."

Mentor replies with a question:
"What is superior then?
Art or money?"

Mentee replies in moments:
"All that you don't have
will embrace you as art,
All that you have
will help you in selling that art."

"Is it then a case of
superiority versus inferiority?
Or, a case of,
co-existential equation of heterogeneity?"

Mentor replies to Mentee,
a smiling face smiley
and writes,
"You, my friend,
have come far…
No more, I, the Mentor;
nor Mentee you are!
Be a mirror to me
and to many others—
I can absolutely declare
now that ready you are!"

Mentee replies with a smile
and folding hands of gratitude:
"Sir! You shall forever
remain my pathfinding North Star!
Even when heterogeneously
we go miles and miles far!"

DON'T KNOW. BEAUTIFULLY.

Mentee asks Mentor,
"How long is a story?
What is the right focus?"

Mentor replies,
"Every moment is a story.
There is no right or wrong focus.
You just
happen to develop
your own perspective."

Curious Mentee once again,
"How to picture an illusion then?"

Mentor with a contented smile,
"I don't know, my friend!
I don't know. Beautifully."

"Is it an unnecessary question?"
—reacted Mentee.

"No.
Not at all.
You asked the most beautiful question.
Now invest your life.
Invest
to enjoy
finding the answer,"
—responded Mentor.

"But I see a blurry picture, Sir!"

"If you see it blurry, that is okay.
Your life codes are hidden treasures.
Decode them."

"How Sir? How do I go about that?"
Mentee did not ask vocally.
Curious eyes only speaking.

"Observe.
Absorb.
Seek.
Find.
Give away."
Mentor says with closed eyes.

And continues,
"As you sit,
see,
run,
fly,
feel,
touch down,
you will feel pain."

"Pain?"
—murmured Mentee.

"Yes. Pain.
But, your pain
is not going to be the only gain.
Your clarity
will come from your clouds."
Mentor opens his eyes.

Mentee's eyes lit up and they ask again,
"You articulated this to me so clearly!
Why do you say that you don't know, Sir?"

Mentor closes his eyes once again.
Smiles at Mentee.
Both their faces radiate.
A few lines
come out from him
like a hymn—
"A blanket of fog led the way
and it said:
Clarity is a well-oiled machine.
Ambiguity is humane.
Keep at it.
Keep on keeping on.
I still don't know, my friend.
Don't know. Beautifully."

POETS OF SURRENDER

You cannot capture
everything as it is.
The moments ask,
“Why is there a hurry to capture?”

Why prepare for memories to remain?
Let moments be free birds…
Just embrace—
don’t kill to capture.

See, sense, smell, touch, taste, feel;
Don’t try to memorize.
Forget with humaneness.
What remains becomes poetry.

Whether you write
or paint
or sing
or film
or play
or cook
or make love
or just be—
some rare things happen
in moments of total surrender…
Cannot be calculated or intellectualized
even him or herself by the creator!

… … …

Poets are as young as they want to be,
as old as they need to be.

… … …

We are all born poets, in our ways,
of something or the other;
some are reborn, in search of simplicity,
as the poets of surrender.

UNPLANNED TRIPS

Holy smokes that the soul gave up on,
did not give up on the self.
It left a cruel migraine
and left a divine crack.

Light comes in through there
leading onto an Aeonian cave…
Nowhere else do I plan my trips for,
nowhere else do I see you blessed more.

Trips to jungles, hills, oceans, rivers,
sunrises, sunsets, moonlights, stars—
where not?
Cities, villages, posh plush, simpletons,
strangers, lovers, friends, associates—
with whom not?

In my urban life's pleasures and struggles,
not a monk I am, but a wanderer wayfarer self;
Many selves that I have seen within
as I dived in to break the "I" in my own self.

Selves setting out
on trips unplanned,
bringing stardust galore
to travel some more.
Now I need not the holy smoke
or joyful drink anymore,
as they long gave me
what we were truly meant for.

Temples, mosques, churches, gurdwaras,
namghars, monasteries, pagodas—
they became one;
So became one self of ‘we’ from the selves of ‘I’
and we became one in all,
while becoming all in one.

THE ROADS TAUGHT
EP:1

The roads taught:
Don't try
to
master your shadow.
Don't try
to be
that ego
which tries to control.
Rather,
try and be
that ego
which takes a shadow
as the self's mirror of the moment.

THE ROADS TAUGHT EP:2

The roads taught via an elderly couple
running a small humble tea-stall:

Delete from your memories
all that you think you have done for others:
a favour, a help, a lending, a sacrifice—
delete them all.
Instead, keep in your mind
what others have done for you:
a favour, a help, a lending, a sacrifice—
keep them in mind.

Life is not about or not to be made of
bargaining over who owes you what—
but about being grateful,
inside of you,
and remaining so.

....

....

THE ROADS TAUGHT
EP:3

With placards double their size,
the children met on the roads taught:

....
Carbon's home
Oxygen for free
Gift a plant
Plant a tree
....

Highways, housings,
City, markets grow
Industrial plants are
Never running slow

Soaring heat and
Polluted air
Passing the blame
Not at all fair

Must and now we
Plant some trees
Not only plant but
Care for them trees

Not for a day or
Not PR, pictures
But for a world worth
Many pretty pictures

………
Gift a plant
Plant a tree
Water the plant
Feed the tree
………

………
Carbon's home
Oxygen for free
Gift a plant
Plant a tree
………

THE ROADS TAUGHT EP:4

Discriminations taught:

Work with your hands—
You are a labourer.
Work with your hands and head—
You are a craftsman.
Work with your hands, head and heart—
You are an artist.

The roads rectified:

From a daydreamer—
to a dreamer,
onto a doer—
Hands that put in the labour,
Head that knows the need of labour,
Heart that loves being a labourer—
You remain a mere daydreamer,
Until respecting labour.

WHAT IS YOUR FEAR?

A frail grey-haired old woman
and a beautiful young woman,
in conversation,
waiting for their train to arrive.

Young woman: What is your fear?
Old woman: None.
Young woman: Is that even possible?
Old woman: Why not?

Young woman: I mean, how can you be free
from all fears?

Old woman: We are passengers,
young friend.
There is birth—at one end.
There is death—at the other.
....
If made into a spiral,
that comes and goes around,
it stretches
into a road of birth,
death,
and rebirth.
Where is the scope for fear?
Tell me, my friend,
why should I have any fear?
....

Both women looked at each other
with poignant silence.
An air whistle sound coming in
made felt its presence.
Their train appeared shortly,
a cacophony hugged the station.
People living parallel lives boarded the train,
like a human-train procession…

EACH NIGHT A DAY IS BORN

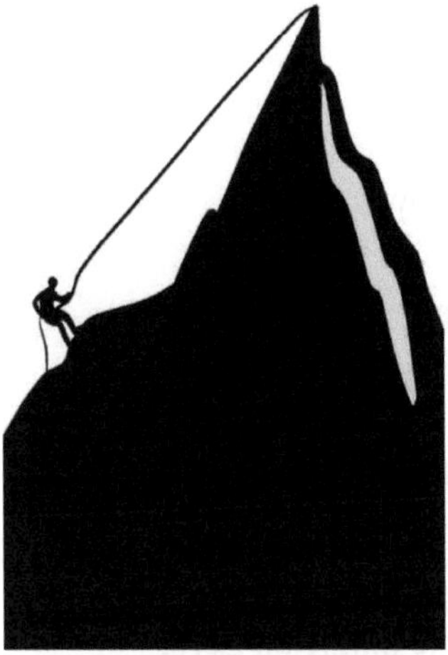

All roads do take you somewhere…
You don't ever take any road anywhere.

Who stopped you
from doing
all that you wished you did?
Directly or indirectly,
disguised in excuses,
it's you and only you
who did stop you.

Learning and unlearning,
aren't they on an orbital loop?
Knowledge and wisdom,
why keep entangled with a hook?
Resting on laurels
why is the mind now?
Improving as a fool
are you much fooler now?

Why don't you get up,
get going and try taking a road somewhere?
Don't you believe—
no one is nobody and everyone is somebody!

Travel between minus and plus effortlessly
like the forever humble magician Zero,
Division and multiplication, leave all to destiny
like the forever humble magician Zero.

Walls shall make ways
For doors and windows—
Or else where would the stories be?
Where else would tomorrow be?
Light would come in through…
Darkness would let in too…
Each night a day is born,
For you and I to be reborn.
Each night a day is born,
For you and I to be reborn.

Thank you

for

being till here

or

starting from here...

THANK YOU! :))

Printed by Libri Plureos GmbH in Hamburg,
Germany

9 789363 318021